EDGE
BOOKS

THE KIDS' GUIDE TO

Robots

BY BARBARA J. DAVIS

Consultant:
Reid Simmons, PhD
Carnegie Mellon University
Robotics Institute

Capstone
press

Mankato, Minnesota

Edge Books are published by Capstone Press,
151 Good Counsel Drive, P.O. Box 669, Mankato, Minnesota 56002.
www.capstonepress.com

Books published by Capstone Press are manufactured with paper
containing at least 10 percent post-consumer waste.

Library of Congress Cataloging-in-Publication Data
Davis, Barbara J., 1952 –
    The kids' guide to robots / by Barbara J. Davis.
    p. cm. — (Edge books. Kids' guides)
    Includes bibliographical references and index.
    Summary: "Describes a wide variety of robots and their applications,
including history and current research" — Provided by publisher.
    ISBN 978-1-4296-3368-0 (library binding)
    1. Robots — Juvenile literature. I. Title. II. Series.
TJ211.2.D392 2010
629.8'92 — dc22   2009010960

Editorial Credits
Gillia Olson, editor; Veronica Bianchini, designer; Eric Gohl, media researcher

Photo Credits
Alamy/K-PHOTOS, 11 (middle); The London Art Archive, 6
AP Images/Dima Gavrysh, 21 (top); Mike Derer, 20; PA Wire/David Parry, 19 (bottom); PA
    Wire/Peter Byrne, 26 (bottom); Stanley Leary, 9 (middle)
Art Life Images/Plus Pix, 11 (top)
Courtesy of American Honda Motor Co. Inc., cover (ASIMO), 5, 25 (both)
DARPA, 28
DVIC/Cherie Cullen, 17 (top right); LCPL Donavan Miskell, 17 (top left); Master Sgt.
    Robert W. Valenca, 16 (inset); Sgt. 1st Class Michael Guillory, 16
Getty Images Inc./AFP/Major Fromentin, 14; AFP/Toshifumi Kitamura, 17 (bottom); AFP/
    Yoshikazu Tsuno, 8, 18, 22; Bongarts/Malte Christians, 23 (bottom); Brandi Simons, 21
    (bottom); Junko Kimura, 27; Koichi Kamoshida, 29 (bottom); Library of Congress, 7
    (top); Popperfoto, 5 (inset); WireImage/Jeffrey Mayer, 4 (left)
iStockphoto/Matjaz Boncina, 19 (top); Ricardo Azoury, 10 (bottom)
NASA, 12; Jet Propulsion Laboratory, 13
Photo Researchers Inc./Hank Morgan, 9 (top); Peter Menzel, 7 (bottom), 15 (bottom); Sam
    Ogden, 26 (top)
Shutterstock/Baloncici, 10 (top); Fotocrisis, cover (nanobot), 29 (top); Michelle Marsan,
    cover (auto factory); riekephotos, 23 (top); SFC, 4 (right)
University of Illinois at Urbana-Champaign/Department of Agricultural & Biological
    Engineering, 11 (bottom)
Velodyne Lidar Inc., 9 (bottom)
Woods Hole Oceanographic Institution/Photo by Chris Linder, 15 (top)

TABLE OF CONTENTS

Not Just Science Fiction

When you hear "robot," what comes to mind?
A barrel-shaped, beeping, whistling robot like R2-D2?
Or maybe one that seems almost human, like C-3PO?
These robots from Star Wars are science fiction. But
robots are not just science fiction anymore.

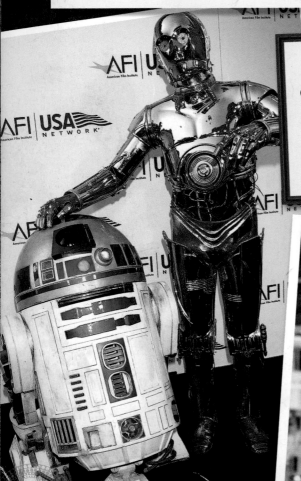

Robots are a very real part of
our world. Robots work in factories
putting products together. Other
robots help do surgeries in hospitals.
Some robots even play sports.

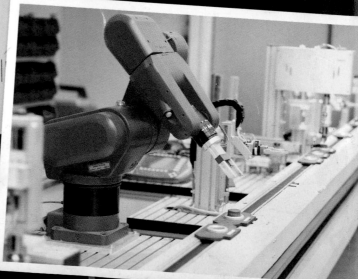

What is a "robot" exactly? A true robot is a machine that can sense the world and make a decision based on what it senses. Most people also use the word "robot" to describe machines that are controlled remotely by people.

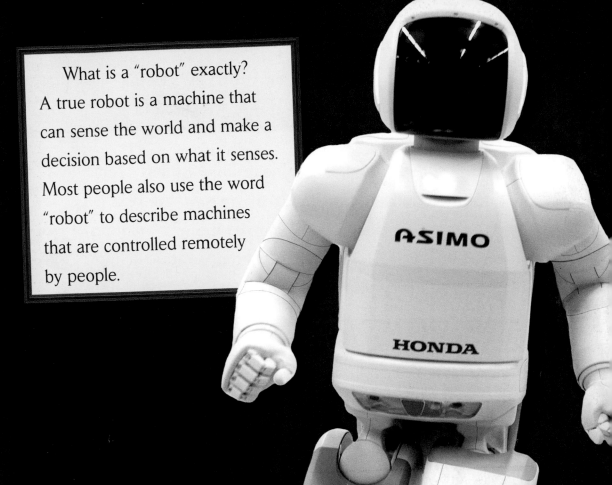

THE WORD "ROBOT"

In 1920, Karel Capek wrote a play about artificial beings that looked and acted like humans. Scientists created them to do jobs in factories that people didn't want to do. Capek called them *robota*, which means "forced work" in the Czech language. The word became "robot" in English.

Robot History

The idea of a humanlike machine to do work has been around for thousands of years. A Greek myth in the *Iliad*, written between 800 and 700 BC, may be the first mention of a "robot." The god Hephaestus makes a bronze statue, Talos, come to life. Below are other important events in robot history.

400 BC: Greek scientist Archytas of Tarentum builds a wooden pigeon. This automaton was able to fly in small circles. Experts think the bird's wings flapped up and down on jets of air.

AD 1100s: Abu al-Jazari builds automata that play musical instruments. Changes in water pressure cause the musicians to move.

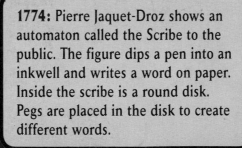

1774: Pierre Jaquet-Droz shows an automaton called the Scribe to the public. The figure dips a pen into an inkwell and writes a word on paper. Inside the scribe is a round disk. Pegs are placed in the disk to create different words.

1947: ENIAC, the first electronic computer, is put into use. It fills an entire room. Computers give rise to robots as they are known today.

1948: Scientist W. Grey Walter builds a turtle-shaped robot called Elmer. It senses light and when it bumps something. The robot then corrects its movement, becoming the first robot to make decisions.

1961: The world's first working robot joins the General Motors' auto assembly line. UNIMATE handles and stacks hot metal.

1971: Intel introduces the first microprocessor. One tiny chip is as powerful as ENIAC. Microprocessors give robots much greater computing power.

1993: Rodney Brooks begins to build Cog. This robot is designed to learn like a child, a "bottom-up" style of programming.

2005: Stanford University wins the Grand Challenge. This car race gave a prize to makers of the first autonomous robot car to complete a course. The car drove itself!

automaton — a mechanical device designed to follow set operations; the plural of automaton is automata.

autonomous — not under anyone's control; autonomous robots are not operated by remote control.

HOW ROBOTS SENSE THE WORLD

How does a robot know where it's going? How can a machine hear? Robots use sensors to gather information. The sensors send electrical signals back to the robot's "brain," which is its central processing unit. The robot can then act on the information.

Hearing

Microphones and other electronic tools act as the robot's ears. Robot sensors can be much more sensitive than human ears.

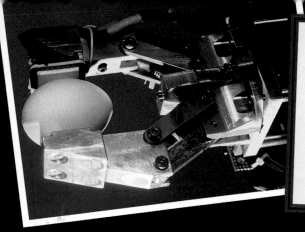

Touch

Bump sensors tell a robot when it bumps something. Pressure sensors tell a robot when it has touched something and how hard to press.

Sight

Infrared sensors are used with infrared light. The robot shines the light. The light bounces off walls and objects, showing the robot where to steer. Sonar uses sound waves in the same way. LIDAR (Light Detection and Ranging) sensors also use lasers in a similar way.

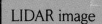

LIDAR image

Smell

Artificial noses have sensors that detect certain smells, such as smoke or poisonous chemicals.

infrared — light waves that aren't seen by a person's naked eye
laser — a thin, intense, high-energy beam of light

ROBOTS IN INDUSTRY

What's the difference between a robot and a machine like a dishwasher? The robot can be programmed to do other jobs. Dishwashers will only wash dishes.

Nearly everything you wear or use has come in contact with a robot. Robots may have tightened a screw, painted it, or packed it in a box.

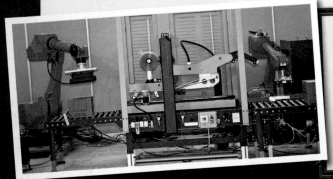

Shipping and Packing

Robots are often used to pack things into boxes. Other robots pick up boxes of goods and load them on trucks.

Dangerous Jobs

Robots keep humans out of harm's way by doing dangerous work. Some robots weld, like these robots in the automobile industry.

Quality Control

Robots can look for problems in a product. They use sensors to watch for irregular products coming off an assembly line.

Working with Sensitive Materials

Robots are clean. They don't shed skin or hair like people do. For this reason, robots often work with sensitive materials. Even specks of dust can harm some electronics.

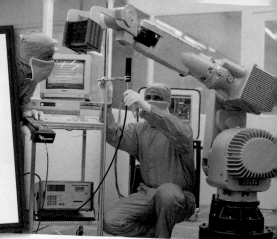

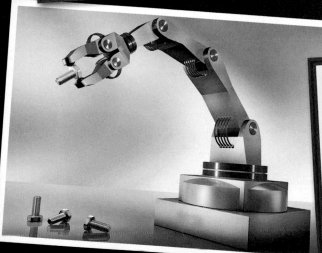

Details

Robot can do very fine work, like tightening small screws and bolts. In the food industry, robots can decorate cakes. Spray painting robots do an even finish every time. Plus, they don't waste paint.

AGANTS

The AgAnt is a small robot designed to work with other AgAnts. They look for weeds. When a weed is found, they signal each other. Then they swarm together and pull out the weed. AgAnts could someday patrol cornfields to keep them weed free.

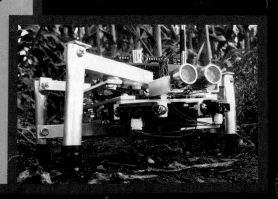

ROBOT EXPLORERS

Space is cold and people can't breathe up there. Humans need a lot of equipment to survive in space. Robots don't have the same problems. They help scientists explore the mysteries of other worlds.

ROBONAUT

NASA is developing Robonaut to help astronauts with daily tasks. This robot has a head, body, arms, and hands with fingers that bend. Robonauts could hand tools to astronauts and prepare work sites. They'll help clean up after the astronauts too.

In January 2004, two robot rovers, Spirit and Opportunity, landed on Mars. Scientists planned for these rovers to explore the planet for 90 days. As of May 2009, these robots are still going.

The robots use their arms to scrape and chip rock samples. Both robots have cameras to take pictures of Mars' surface. The Mars rovers sometimes run on their own. A person on earth sends each robot a message telling it a location to reach. The rovers use their sensors to decide the best path to get there.

Fun Fact:

Spirit and Opportunity found proof that liquid water once flowed on Mars.

Ocean Explorers

You don't need to go to space to find danger. Two-thirds of the earth's surface is covered by water. Most of this area remains unexplored, especially the deep sea. Robot explorers are built to withstand the very high pressure and cold temperatures of the deep sea.

ROVs

Remotely Operated Vehicles (ROVs) can dive to the deepest parts of the ocean. They are controlled remotely. A cable connects them to a power source on a surface ship. ROVs are used for exploring sunken ships, repairing the walls of dams, and fixing oil rigs.

Fun Fact:

There are more than 3,000 ROVs in use throughout the world.

AUVs

Unlike ROVs, Autonomous Underwater Vehicles (AUVs) aren't connected to a power source with a cable. AUVs run on batteries. They are programmed for a mission and carry it out. They are often used to map the seafloor.

A MINE-HUNTING CRAB

A six-legged military robot is being designed to find and explode mines on shorelines. Like a crab, Ariel can move forward, backward, and sideways.

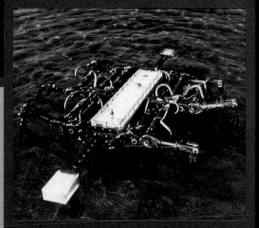

ROBOTS FOR SAFETY

People are always looking for ways to make military and law enforcement jobs safer. Robots are one way to do it. Nearly all robots used in these fields are controlled remotely. People use the robots to help them do dangerous jobs.

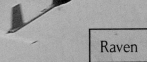

Raven

Pilotless Planes

Flying robots are called Unmanned Aerial Vehicles (UAVs). They range in size. The 5-pound (2.3-kilogram) Raven can be launched by hand. The Reaper is the size of a small passenger plane. UAVs are most often used to take pictures of enemy soldiers and bases. Reapers carry and launch missiles.

Reaper

Ground robots

Unmanned Ground Vehicles (UGVs) stay on the ground. PackBot is a small, tough robot that fits in a soldier's backpack. Military soldiers and bomb squads may use them to explode mines or bombs. The Gladiator system looks like a mini tank. It can have cameras or guns, and it even shoots grenades.

PackBot

Gladiator system

RESCUE ROBOT

The robot Enryu is being designed to do rescue work. Enryu lifts cars. After earthquakes, Enryu could free people trapped in rubble. It is 11.5 feet (3.5 meters) tall and weighs about 10,000 pounds (4,500 kilograms). Its arms can lift about 1,000 pounds (450 kilograms). Enryu means "rescue dragon" in Japanese.

Robots Helping People

Many scientists believe the future of robots is as helpers in the home. How about a robot that can clean your room? Or a robot to take out the trash or mow the lawn?

Wakamaru

Wakamaru is just over 3 feet (.9 meter) tall. This tiny robot recognizes faces. It knows 10,000 words and can have simple conversations with people. Wakamaru was designed to help elderly people. It has built-in features to call for help in an emergency. Wakamaru is not for sale to the public, but it is a step in making robots that are home companions.

Vacuum Cleaners

The Roomba from iRobot has been around for several years. This circular vacuum cleans your floors autonomously. Roombas have sensors to detect dirt. They also bring themselves back to the charger when their battery gets low.

Automower

Lawnmowers

Mowing the lawn can be a big chore. Robotic lawnmowers like Robomower, Automower, and LawnBott are designed to help. They can cut any yard that a regular push mower can cut. Users set up a wire to define the lawn for Robomower. Robomower then stays within the wire.

Robots in Medicine

Robots have been used to help perform medical operations since 1990. Robot hands are steadier than human hands. Plus, surgery robots can go where human hands cannot. They can reach in through tiny cuts in the body and move through blood vessels. They can even move around inside a beating heart!

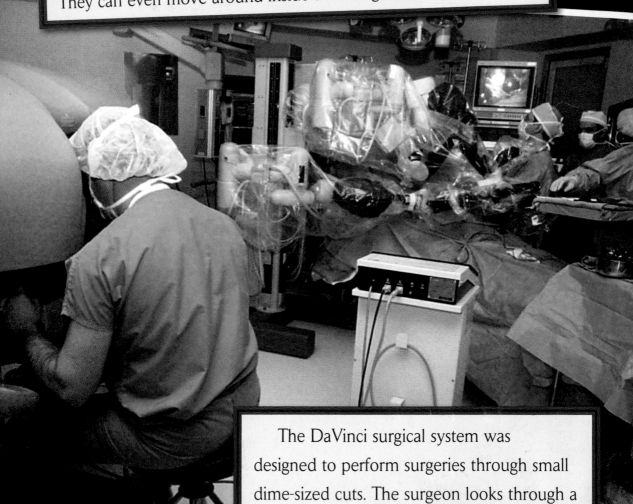

The DaVinci surgical system was designed to perform surgeries through small dime-sized cuts. The surgeon looks through a viewer and uses hand controls to maneuver the system's four robotic arms. A camera magnifies the view of the surgery. These systems cost about $1.5 million.

ROBOT LIMBS

Artificial hands, arms, and legs are being made to work like the real thing. The newest versions in testing work with a person's own nerves and muscles. Artificial arms are being tested that are wired directly into the brain. The goal is that the user will simply think about grabbing something, and the arm will respond.

Fun Fact:

In 2001, doctors in New York performed an operation on a patient in Strasbourg, France. The operation was done by a remote-controlled robot called ZEUS.

ROBOTS FOR FUN

Remote-controlled trucks and planes have been around for years. Maybe you even have one. Today there are robot pets, dolls, and soccer players that have no remote. The newest robot toys use sensors to make decisions.

A Thinking Dinosaur

Put something by Pleo's mouth and it tries to take it and chew. Scratch Pleo under the chin and it makes happy sounds. Sound like a puppy? It's a baby dinosaur. Pleo is one of the newest "smart" robots. These robots can learn. Pleo uses sensors to experience the world and respond to it. The things Pleo learns affect how it acts.

Custom Robots

Several companies sell kits to make your own robot. A popular one is Lego Mindstorms. These kits come with a variety of parts and programmable software. Everything from mini-aircraft to orchestra conductors have been built with these kits. What would your robot do?

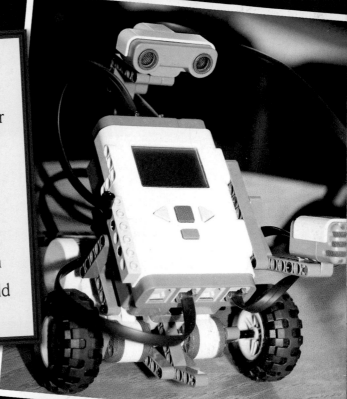

ROBOT SPORTS

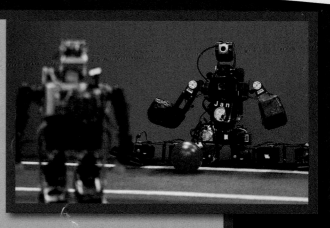

Scientists are using soccer to advance the field of robotics. The RoboCup is held every year. Up to 3,000 robots from 40 countries compete. RoboCup's goal is to have a robot team good enough to beat the human soccer world champions by 2050. The robots are not remote controlled. They have sensors and programming to play by themselves. The robots range from small boxlike robots on wheels to human-looking robots the size of a teenager.

HUMANOIDS AND ANDROIDS

The biggest goal in the robot world is a machine that looks, acts, and talks like a human. Engineers are making startling progress in this area. Humanoid robots have the same general shape as a human but don't look human. Androids look so real, they fool people!

ARTIFICIAL INTELLIGENCE

Artificial intelligence is the ability of a machine to think like a person. Robot makers are trying two different ways of creating artificial intelligence. The "top down" method requires people to program a computer with all the knowledge of a person. The other way is "bottom up." In this method, the robot is programmed to learn. It tries new things and sees the result, much the way children learn.

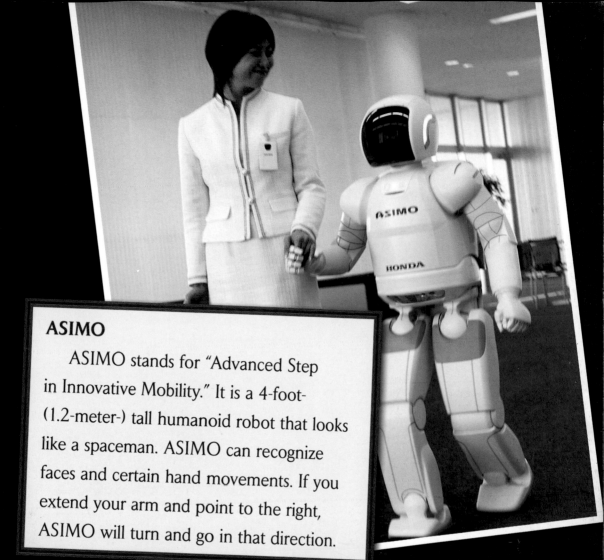

ASIMO

ASIMO stands for "Advanced Step in Innovative Mobility." It is a 4-foot- (1.2-meter-) tall humanoid robot that looks like a spaceman. ASIMO can recognize faces and certain hand movements. If you extend your arm and point to the right, ASIMO will turn and go in that direction.

Fun Fact:

In 2008, ASIMO conducted the Detroit Symphony Orchestra in a special performance.

Leonardo

Although it doesn't look human, Leonardo can be considered a humanoid robot. Leonardo is a cute, furry robot designed to interact with and learn from people. Leonardo learns tasks from human teachers. The makers at Massachusetts Institute of Technology want to create a way for humans to interact normally with a robot.

iCub

Scientists from a group of European universities are working together to create a robot as smart as a 3½-year-old child. Called iCub, this robot will do simple tasks and speak by learning like a child. The group is also making the programming available to anyone interested in trying this type of robotics.

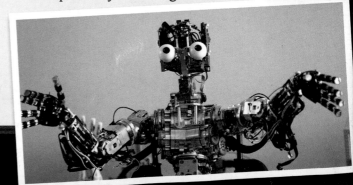

Repliee

Professor Hiroshi Ishiguro of Osaka University has built some of the most human-looking robots in the world. Repliee Q1Expo is an android. The robot has soft silicone "skin." It flutters its eyelashes. Repliee even seems to breathe. Forty-two mechanical devices in its upper body allow it to move.

Future Robots

In the future, robots will likely be a large part of people's everyday lives. Some robots will be almost human in how they look and act. If you can imagine it, scientists are probably working on it right now. Future robots are closer than you think.

Self-Driving Cars

Scientists are making strides in the quest for a self-driving car. The Grand Challenge was a contest for autonomous vehicles. Using sensors and global positioning systems, vehicles had to drive themselves through a desert obstacle course. No vehicles finished the first contest in 2004. But in 2005, a team from Stanford University completed and won the challenge.

The 2007 Urban Challenge course was meant to copy city driving. Tartan Racing, a team including Carnegie Mellon University, General Motors, and others, won the race.

2005 Grand Challenge race

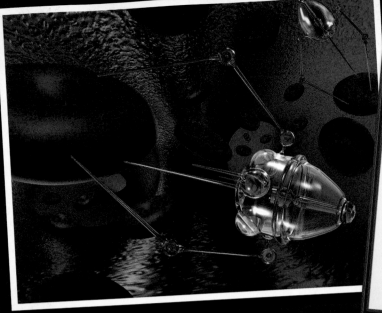

Nanobots

A nanobot is a robot so small you would need a microscope to see it. Imagine robots like these traveling to a diseased human cell. It would be able to destroy the cell without hurting the healthy cells around it.

Cyborgs

What would you do with the strength of 100 men? How about the eyesight of an eagle? Future robots might be a combination of human and robot parts, called a cyborg. A human brain could run a robot body. Or a human could have special robotic arms or legs. Although robotic arms and legs are under study, most scientists think true cyborgs are far in the future.

Glossary

android (AN-droid) — a robot that looks, thinks, and acts like a human being

artificial intelligence (ar-ti-FISH-uhl in-TEL-uh-junss)— the ability of a machine to think like a person

automaton (aw-TAH-muh-tahn) — a mechanical device designed to follow set operations; the plural of automaton is automata.

autonomous (aw-TAH-nuh-muhss) — able to control oneself; autonomous robots are not operated by remote control.

cyborg (CYE-borg) — a being that is a combination of organic and mechanical parts; cyborg is short for cybernetic organism.

humanoid (HYOO-muh-noid) — a robot shaped somewhat like a human but is clearly a robot

infrared (in-fruh-RED) — light waves in the electromagnetic spectrum between visible light and microwaves

laser (LAY-zur) — a thin, intense, high-energy beam of light

nanobot (NAN-oh-baht) — an extremely small robot

weld (WELD) — to join two pieces of metal together by heating them until they melt

READ MORE

Allman, Toney. *From Bug Legs to Walking Robots.* Imitating Nature. Detroit: Kidhaven Press, 2006.

VanVoorst, Jennifer Fretland. *Rise of the Thinking Machines: The Science of Robots.* Headline Science. Minneapolis, Minn.: Compass Point Books, 2008.

Yes Magazine, editor. *Robots: From Everyday to Out of This World.* Tonawanda, N.Y.: Kids Can Press, 2008.

INTERNET SITES

FactHound offers a safe, fun way to find Internet sites related to this book. All of the sites on FactHound have been researched by our staff.

Here's all you do:

Visit *www.facthound.com*

FactHound will fetch the best sites for you!

INDEX